— OUTDOOR ADVENTURE GUIDES —

WILDERNESS SURVIVAL

Basic Safety for Outdoor Adventures

by Blake Hoena

Consultant: Gabriel J. Gassman
Outdoor Professional

CAPSTONE PRESS
a capstone imprint

Capstone Captivate is published by Capstone Press, an imprint of Capstone.
1710 Roe Crest Drive
North Mankato, Minnesota 56003
www.capstonepub.com

Copyright © 2020 Capstone. All rights reserved. No part of this publication may be reproduced in whole or in part, or stored in a retrieval system, or transmitted in any form or by any means, electronic, mechanical, photocopying, recording, or otherwise, without written permission of the publisher.

Cataloging-in-Publication Data is available on the Library of Congress website.
ISBN: 978-1-5435-9029-6 (library binding)
ISBN: 978-1-4966-6615-4 (paperback)
ISBN: 978-1-5435-9030-2 (eBook PDF)

Summary: This guidebook provides basic tips and tricks for surviving in the wilderness, including sheltering against weather extremes, battling bugs, and fending off meddlesome animals.

Editorial Credits
Editor: Kellie M. Hultgren; Designer: Juliette Peters;
Media Researcher: Morgan Walters; Production Specialist: Katy LaVigne

Photo Credits
Capstone Studio: Karon Dubke, background 11, top 35, 44; Dreamstime: Tatabrada, bottom 23; Getty Images: Hero Images, 43, Sollina Images, top 15; iStockphoto: Fertnig, 33, PeopleImages, 1, Tom Merton, left 31; Juliette Peters, top Cover, 22, 28; Shutterstock: AjayTvm, 24, Alan Gordine, bottom left 41, aliaksei kruhlenia, (icons) design element, Arina P Habich, middle left 17, Asmiana, 40, Atovot, 42, Brendt A Petersen, 18, Catalin Petolea, 26, Chelsea Mendenhall, 45, Dmitry Naumov, top right 17, Don Mammoser, 36, DPS, 37, Dudarev Mikhail, 39, Elena Yakusheva, 12, francesco cepolina, 6, GUNDAM_Ai, top 23, hsagencia, bottom right 31, Jakub Janele, 5, Jens Ottoson, top 9, Keith Homan, bottom 25, Lilkin, 32, Little stock, Cover, marla dawn studio, bottom 27, Natvas, bottom left 16, bottom middle 17, Piotr Krzeslak, top right 16, PRESSLAB, Cover, Rachel Juliet Lerch, 30, RobDun, middle 41, Robert Przybysz, 34, saam3rd, (dry leaves) design element, ShaunWilkinson, 19, shutter_o, (moss) Cover, design element, Smit, 20, SolidMaks, bottom 15, Steve Collender, (tape) design element, sunabesyou, 13, Sylvie Bouchard, 10, Tom Grundy, 14, Valentin Valkov, (mat) bottom 21, VBVVCTND, (khaki) design element, Viacheslav Lopatin, top left 41, Volodymyr Krasyuk, bottom 9, wavebreakmedia, 8, Wessel du Plooy, 7, worldofstock, (stump) design element, xpixel, bottom 35, xx85xx, (wood) design element, Yuliia Hurzhos, top 25, ZARIN ANDREY, top 21, zhukovvvlad, bottom 11, Zivica Kerkez, 29; Wikimedia: Daniele Pugliesi, top 27

All internet sites appearing in back matter were available and accurate when this book was sent to press.

TABLE OF CONTENTS

CHAPTER 1
DO NOT PANIC! 4

CHAPTER 2
SHELTER AND FIRE 10

CHAPTER 3
WATER 22

CHAPTER 4
FOOD 28

CHAPTER 5
STAYING SAFE 32

CHAPTER 6
SIGNALING FOR HELP 38

BUILD YOUR OWN SURVIVAL KIT 44

GLOSSARY 46
READ MORE 47
INTERNET SITES 47
INDEX 48

Words in **bold** are in the glossary.

CHAPTER 1
DO NOT PANIC!

Do not panic! That is the number-one rule to remember when it comes to wilderness survival. As long as you are not in immediate danger, remain calm. Take a deep breath and give yourself time to think.

BECOMING UNLOST

As soon as you realize you are lost, stop moving. Do not act until you are calm enough to make smart choices. If you are on a trail, do not leave it. As soon as someone knows you are missing, they will come searching along the trail. Also, the trail likely leads to safety.

If you are not on a trail, stay put! Call for help and listen for a response. Repeat this several times. Stay quiet while listening for a reply. It is as important for you to hear others as it is for them to hear you.

Being lost in the middle of nowhere can be scary. But that is the worst time to let fear take control. Do not rush into action because you are afraid or panicking. In the wild, panic can ruin your chances of survival.

REMEMBER THIS!

Most people are rescued within 12 hours of becoming lost. So the first decisions you make are often the most important. Plan carefully and stay positive!

WHAT'S YOUR SITUATION?

If you are in danger, whether from a wild animal, severe weather, or some other threat, get to safety.

When you are safe, **observe** your surroundings. Are you on a hillside or by a river? Are there trees nearby? Are you on a sandy beach? Is it a sunny day or a stormy one? Is the temperature warm or cool?

Use what you see to make smart choices. If you are stranded on a sunny beach, seek shade to avoid sunburn and overheating. If temperatures are cool, build a fire before it gets colder at night.

What do you observe in this place?

Next, make a mental list of what you have on hand. Do you have any food or water? Do you have matches to make a fire? A tarp for shelter? Consider the possible uses for every item you can see.

SAFETY TIP

Before you go on an outdoor adventure, always tell someone where you are going and when you plan to be back. If anything goes wrong, someone will know when and where to start looking for you.

THE RULE OF THREE

When you are safe, you can think about what to do next. Use the rule of three to make a plan. You need three things to survive for short periods of time:

- Oxygen (in the air you breathe)
- Shelter, including clothing and fire
- Sustenance, which is food and water

These three needs come first. Which is most important? The second part of the rule of three helps you decide. It states that people can survive for around:

- 3 minutes without oxygen or in freezing water
- 3 hours in extreme weather
- 3 days without water
- 3 weeks without food

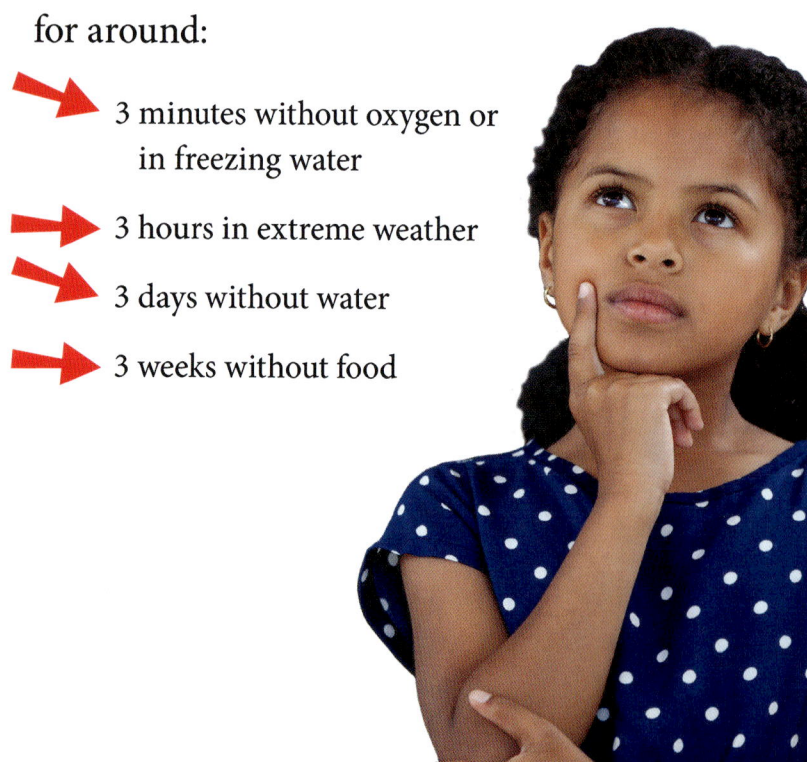

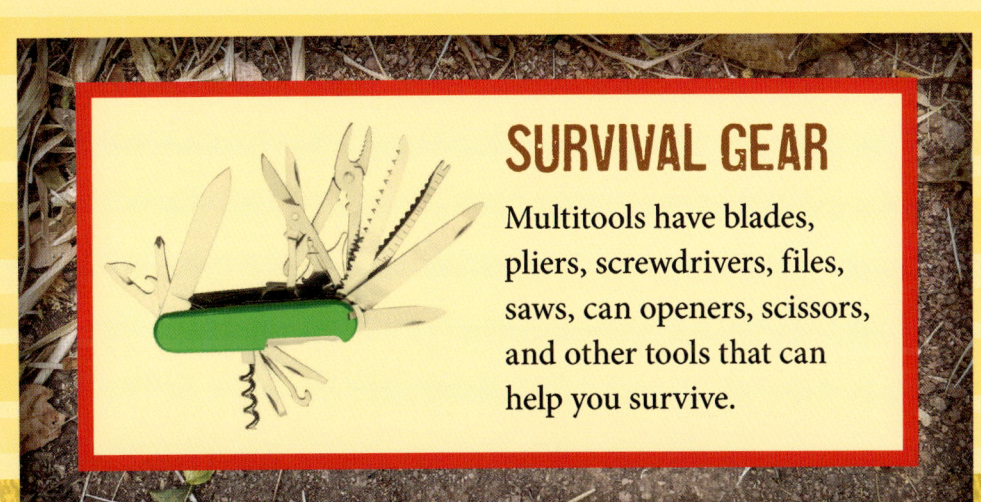

SURVIVAL GEAR

Multitools have blades, pliers, screwdrivers, files, saws, can openers, scissors, and other tools that can help you survive.

CHAPTER 2
SHELTER AND FIRE

Weather may be the greatest threat you face in the wild. Extremely hot temperatures can be just as dangerous as freezing cold temperatures. You need to seek shelter from the weather.

On sunny days, shade is important. The sun's heat will cause you to sweat and lose water. That puts you in danger of becoming **dehydrated**. In extreme cold, you are at risk of **hypothermia** and **frostbite**. These conditions can make it difficult for you to do even simple tasks. They can also be deadly.

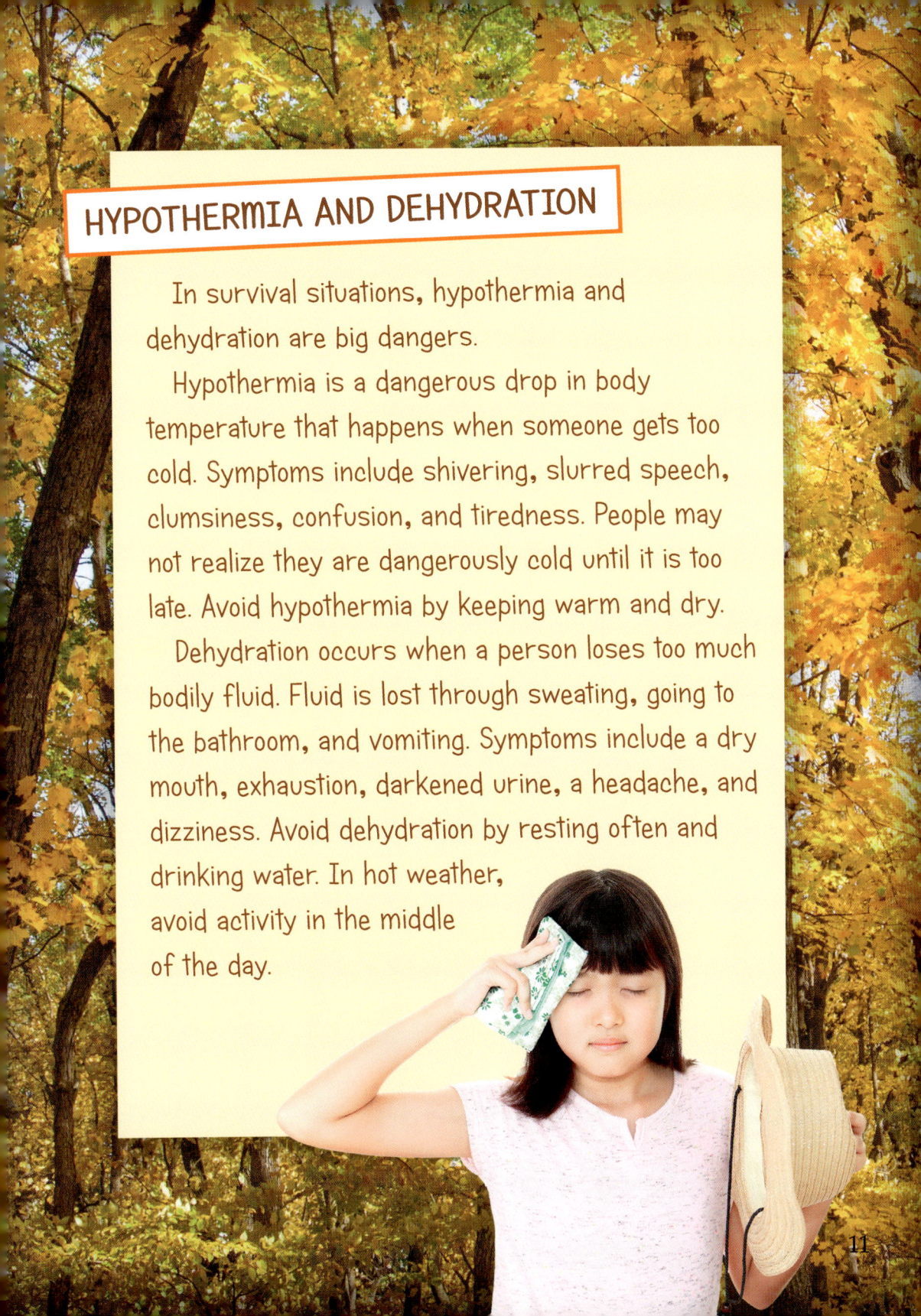

HYPOTHERMIA AND DEHYDRATION

In survival situations, hypothermia and dehydration are big dangers.

Hypothermia is a dangerous drop in body temperature that happens when someone gets too cold. Symptoms include shivering, slurred speech, clumsiness, confusion, and tiredness. People may not realize they are dangerously cold until it is too late. Avoid hypothermia by keeping warm and dry.

Dehydration occurs when a person loses too much bodily fluid. Fluid is lost through sweating, going to the bathroom, and vomiting. Symptoms include a dry mouth, exhaustion, darkened urine, a headache, and dizziness. Avoid dehydration by resting often and drinking water. In hot weather, avoid activity in the middle of the day.

Shelter also gives you a safe place to rest. If it looks like you won't be rescued soon, you need somewhere to recover your energy. When you are tired and suffering from **exhaustion**, you think less clearly. When you need to sleep or take a break from the weather, curl up in your shelter. It helps you stay dry and keeps you out of extreme heat or cold.

REMEMBER THIS!

If you face a wilderness emergency, finding shelter and building a fire will likely be first on your list. A shelter protects you from the weather. A fire can keep you warm, cook food, and help rescuers find you.

SAFETY TIP

Learn to use a compass and a paper map. A paper map of your area will help if you get lost. The GPS on a smartphone might not work in remote places. And if the phone's battery dies, you may not have a place to recharge it.

BUILD YOUR SHELTER

First, decide where to build your shelter. Use your observations to find a safe place. The wrong location can be unsafe or ruin hours of hard work.

Do not build too close to water. On an ocean beach, a shelter might get washed away by the changing tide. Also, beaches can be hot and full of biting bugs.

Low-lying areas can be wet and muddy, which means bugs, bugs, bugs! Also, a sudden storm could flood your shelter.

Pick somewhere dry and protected from the wind. Hillsides and areas with trees are good places to build shelters.

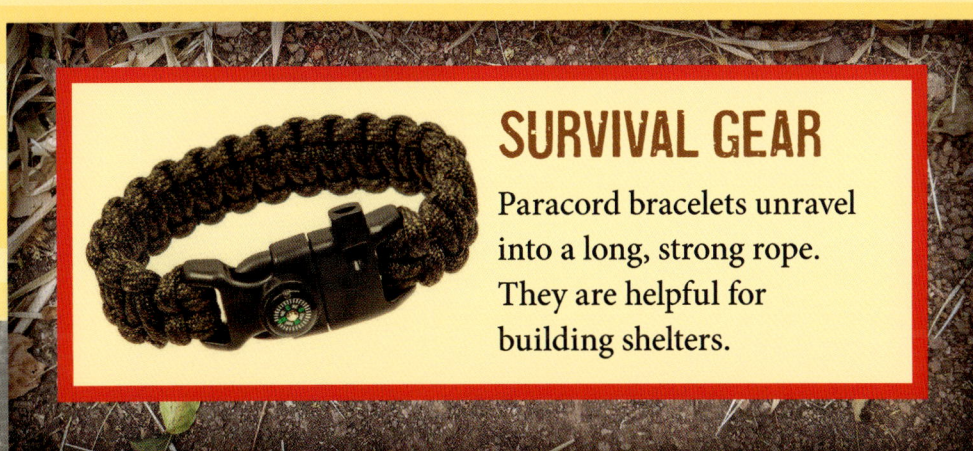

SURVIVAL GEAR

Paracord bracelets unravel into a long, strong rope. They are helpful for building shelters.

TYPES OF SHELTERS

You can build several types of shelter out in the wild. The best type will depend on the materials you have on hand.

A cave is a ready-made shelter. It gets you out of the wind and rain. But caves are often cold, damp, and dark. They might have sudden drops or slippery loose rock. Animals, such as snakes and bears, make caves their homes. Before using a cave as shelter, be sure it is dry and critter free.

A tarp shelter is easy to build. You just need a rope or stick and a covering, such as a tarp or poncho. Tie the rope or stick tightly between two trees. Then hang the covering over it to form a roof. Hold down the edges of the covering with rocks or sticks.

If you do not have a tarp, build a lean-to. Find a fallen tree or tree branch that sits a few feet off the ground. This is your base. Lean branches against it at a 45-degree angle. Then cover the branches with evergreen boughs or leaves and sticks to block out the wind.

If you are lost in the snowy wilderness during the winter, make a snow cave or trench shelter. This protects you from the wind. It also traps body heat inside the hole to help you stay warm. But be careful! A snowy roof can collapse and cut off your air if you don't build your cave properly. And stay away from steep slopes, where avalanches can occur.

REMEMBER THIS!

A bed of leaves and fallen pine boughs inside your shelter will shield you from the cold ground.

STARTING A FIRE

A fire gives you the light and warmth you need to survive. To start a fire, you need matches, a lighter, or a fire-starter kit. Then you need to gather **tinder**, such as scraps of paper, leaves, wood chips, scraps of bark, pine needles, and twigs. To keep a fire going after it is started, you will need fuel, such as larger sticks and logs.

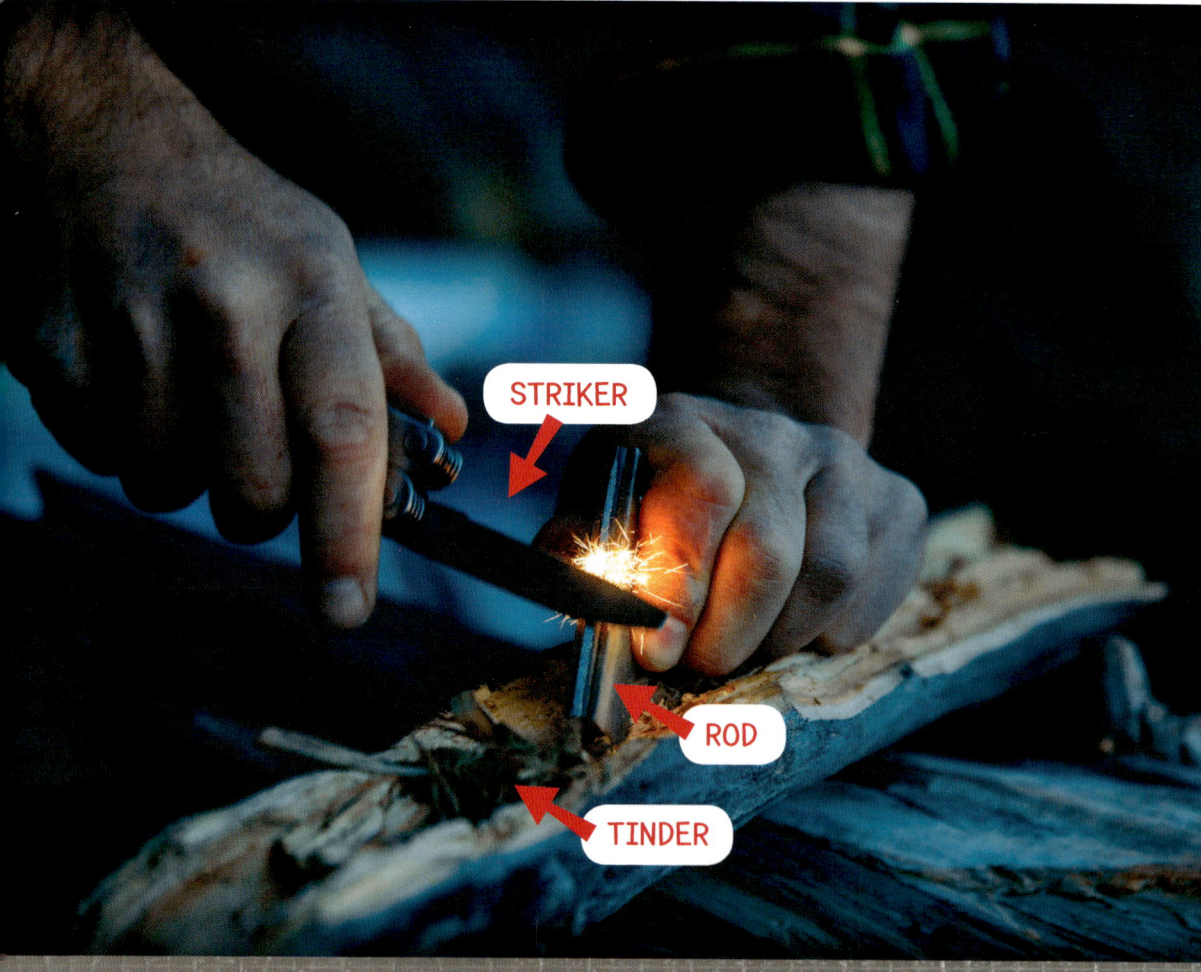

USING A FIRE-STARTER KIT

1. Prepare a clean, dry place outside your shelter to build your fire. Make sure that nothing around or above you can accidentally catch fire.
2. Make a pile of small bits of tinder.
3. Hold the rod at a 45-degree angle while pressing it firmly against the ground near your tinder.
4. Press the edge of the striker against the rod and flick it downward. This will create sparks. If no sparks appear, try pressing a bit harder. When you get sparks, aim them at your tinder.
5. Flick sparks until the tinder begins to smolder and burn. You may need to blow gently on it to grow the flames.
6. Slowly add larger bits of tinder. Adding it too fast can make your fire go out.
7. As the fire grows, add small sticks and then larger pieces of fuel.
8. Keep your fire small. Large fires need more fuel and are more likely to get out of control.

STAYING DRY

Wearing wet clothes is uncomfortable. But during a survival situation, it can also be dangerous. Even in mild temperatures, wet clothes can lead to hypothermia.

If you get wet, change into dry clothes immediately. If you don't have dry clothes, warm up and dry off by your fire. If you can't get a fire going, take your clothes off and wring them out. Once you're dressed again, seek shelter.

If you are chilled, never lie on the bare ground. Cold from the ground will only chill you more. Lie on some sort of padding, whether it's dry leaves, a sleeping pad, or a jacket. Then cover yourself the best you can.

CHAPTER 3
WATER

The rule of three says you can survive about three days without water. You are likely to be rescued before that time runs out. But always keep in mind the need for water.

Water is especially important in extreme weather and when you are very active. When you sweat, you are losing water. If you are working hard or it is hot, pause often for a drink. You may need water sooner than you do in cool weather or while resting. Finding water may even be more important than building a shelter.

REMEMBER THIS!

Just because you found water does not mean that it is safe to drink. **Microorganisms** living in lake and river water can make you sick. If possible, boil water for at least one minute and then let it cool before drinking.

COLLECTING WATER

If you are not near a freshwater lake or river, there are other ways of getting water out in the wild. Rain is one great source. You can use empty containers, like water bottles, cooking pans, and tin cans, to collect rain.

You can also use a tarp or poncho to collect drinking water. Tie it between three or four trees. Place a rock in the middle of the tarp so the rain will form a pool. Then fill any containers you have with the water that collects in it.

SURVIVAL GEAR

Water purification tablets kill the microorganisms in river and lake water, making it safe to drink.

MAKE A SOLAR STILL

A **solar still** can collect water for you even in dry places. It can also make dirty or salty water drinkable. All you need is a sheet of plastic (like a plastic bag), a rock, and something to hold water.

1. Find an area that gets a lot of sunlight, yet where the ground is moist.
2. Dig a hole at least twice as deep as your water container.
3. Place your container at the bottom of the hole.
4. Cover the hole with the plastic sheet.
5. Place rocks and dirt around the edge of the sheet to hold it in place.
6. Put a rock in the middle of the plastic so that it hangs down over the container.

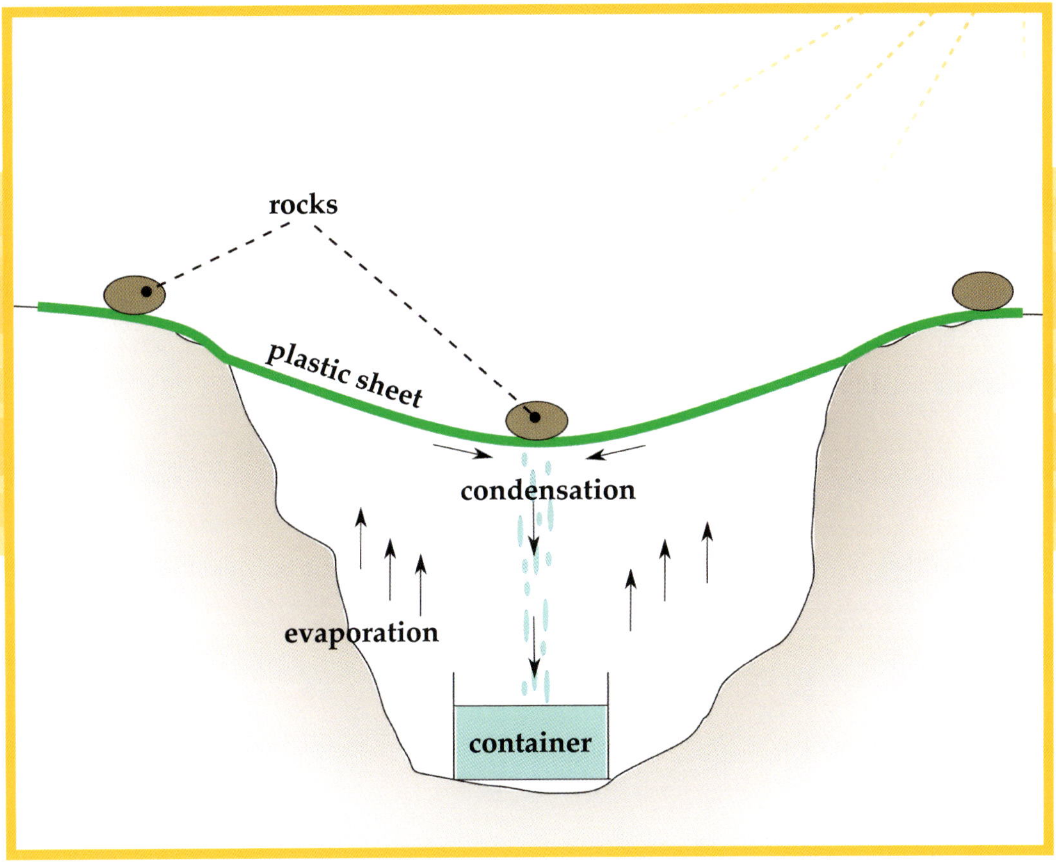

Sunlight will cause the moisture from the ground to condense on the bottom of the plastic and drip into your container. A solar still is slow, but the water it collects is clean.

SURVIVAL GEAR

Coffee filters remove dirt and other things from water. After boiling water or using purification tablets, pour the purified water through the filter to make it even cleaner for drinking.

CHAPTER 4
FOOD

After a couple of hours without a snack, your stomach might begin to grumble. You may think you are starving. But most people are rescued within hours of getting lost. While that is a long time to go between snacks, your body can go much longer without a meal.

Remember the rule of three. You can survive up to three weeks without food. You will only need to search for food if you have been lost for several days.

SAFETY TIP

The smell of any food you have with you could attract animals. If you have a rope and a bag, hang your food from the branch of a tree that is at least 200 feet (61 meters) away from your shelter and at least 15 feet (5 meters) high.

BRING A SNACK

The best way to prepare for a wilderness emergency is to bring safe food with you. Even if you are going on a short adventure, bring a snack, such as granola or an energy bar. Hunger can lead to exhaustion and make it hard to think clearly. And without food, it will take you longer to finish tasks, from setting up a shelter to building a fire.

REMEMBER THIS!

Hunger makes you feel more tired and think less clearly. Take a lot of breaks. The more rested you are, the more alert you will be. When you are alert, you can react to danger faster.

FORAGING

Do not **forage** for food unless you are familiar with the plants in an area. Many can be **toxic**. It's best to avoid eating anything unless you know it is safe. Being hungry is safer than getting sick.

Some common plants, such as dandelion and clover, are edible. You can eat the leaves and flowers of both. But if you wish to forage for food, bring a field guide of edible plants with you. Otherwise it can be too risky.

If you see an animal eating a seed or berry, that does not mean it is safe for you to eat. Animals can eat berries that are toxic to people.

If you truly need food, it is better to eat insects and worms. Bugs are highly nutritious! You might think they are gross, but bugs are safer than plants that might make you ill.

SURVIVAL GEAR

Fishing kits include strong fishing line, a couple of fishhooks, and fishing weights. It is also good to bring artificial bait.

CHAPTER 5
STAYING SAFE

Out in the wild, you will not have a hospital or drug store nearby. Play it safe. Survival situations are not the time to be daring. Avoid taking risks that could lead to injuries. Even a simple cut or a twisted ankle can threaten your chances of survival.

SURVIVAL GEAR

First aid kits are a must. Buy one or assemble your own. If you use something from the kit, replace it as soon as you get home.

FIRST AID

Injuries will happen. Treat cuts and scrapes with serious care. You are at a greater risk of infections out in the wild. Clean injuries out as best you can and apply antibiotic cream from your first aid kit.

If you hurt or break your arm, you can loop a belt or length of rope around your neck to use as a sling.

If you hurt or break your leg, you can tie sturdy sticks on either side of your leg to use as a splint.

WILD ANIMALS

Most wild animals have a natural fear of people. Let them know you are there, and they will probably avoid you. Make noise. Talk. Clap your hands. Animals are most dangerous when they are surprised and feel threatened.

If a wild animal threatens you, don't run away. Instead, raise your arms up in the air. Make yourself look big and scary. Shout and yell. Then slowly back away as you make more noise. Be sure to peek behind you to make sure you don't trip or fall as you walk. When the animal is out of sight, you can turn around and keep moving away.

REMEMBER THIS!

Never run from a predator, such as a bear or mountain lion. If you do, it might mistake you for prey and give chase. And you will never outrun it.

CHAPTER 6
SIGNALING FOR HELP

After you are safe and sheltered, start thinking of being rescued. But don't go looking for help. Instead, help people find you. You can do this through different types of **signals**.

Many hiking survival kits include some kind of signal. One example is safety flares. These chemical sticks burn brightly for a short period of time. You light them when you see a rescuer. But if you didn't bring an emergency signal, you can use things you find in the wild.

REMEMBER THIS!
The more you move around, the more difficult it will be for rescuers to find you. As long as you are not in danger, stay in one place. Otherwise, you might accidently head farther away from help.

TYPES OF SIGNALS

Use several methods to signal for help. Do not rely on just one. Using at least two will make it easier for others to find you.

Build a signal fire. In an open area, build a fire with plenty of fuel. Once it is roaring, place wet leaves and sticks on top. Damp fuel creates lots of smoke. The smoke will rise into the air and be seen for miles around. But do not use a signal fire if wildfire danger in your area is high.

Use a signal mirror. Your compass may have one. But any shiny material can reflect light toward a plane or ship, or someone in the distance. This includes tinfoil, scraps of metal, the bottom of a can, or a smartphone screen.

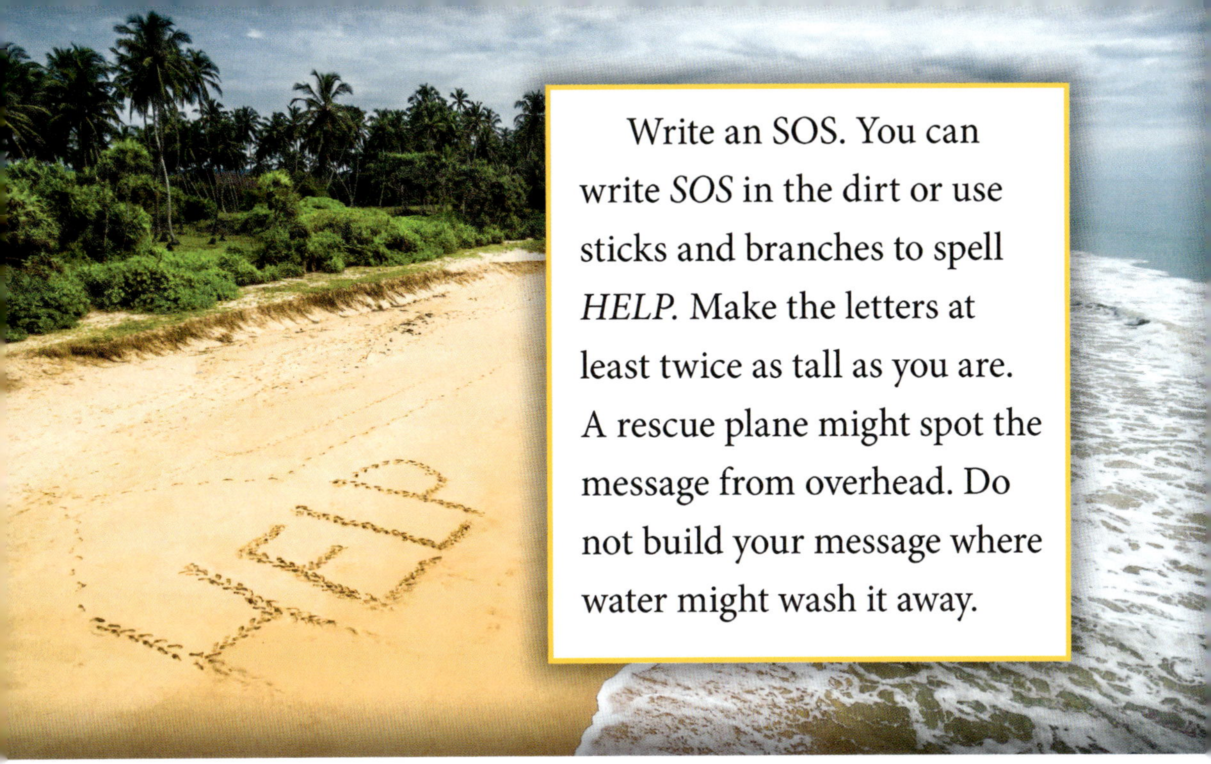

Write an SOS. You can write *SOS* in the dirt or use sticks and branches to spell *HELP.* Make the letters at least twice as tall as you are. A rescue plane might spot the message from overhead. Do not build your message where water might wash it away.

Make a flag. Tie a strip of cloth, a T-shirt, or a spare piece of clothing to the end of a long stick. Set the stick in a place where it might be seen by rescuers.

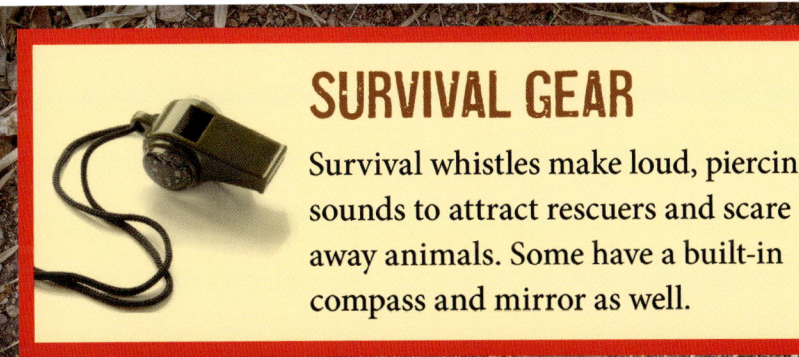

SURVIVAL GEAR

Survival whistles make loud, piercing sounds to attract rescuers and scare away animals. Some have a built-in compass and mirror as well.

PRACTICE, PRACTICE, PRACTICE!

Reading about survival skills is one thing. Putting them to use is another. Do not wait until you are in a life-or-death situation to test the skills you learned in this book. Practice them!

Remember to tell someone before you go on an adventure. Bring a snack and water to keep your body properly fueled and hydrated. Pack clothes to protect yourself from the elements. Don't forget a map and a first aid or survival kit.

Try building a shelter in your backyard with a tarp and some rope. With an adult's help, learn to build a fire with a fire-starter kit. Test your fishing kit in a local pond or river. If you catch a keeper, have an adult show you how to clean and cook it.

Knowing how to survive in the great outdoors is a useful skill. But being prepared is even more helpful. Practice will give you the confidence you need to enjoy many more outdoor adventures!

BUILD YOUR OWN SURVIVAL KIT

Survival kits are useful to have around. You can build a simple one with a small container, like a metal tin. A water bottle holds even more survival supplies. Useful items include:

- ❏ button compass
- ❏ mini flashlight with batteries
- ❏ mini multitool
- ❏ paracord bracelet
- ❏ sheet of tinfoil or zip-close bag
- ❏ 2 water purification tablets
- ❏ whistle

FIRE-STARTING EQUIPMENT
- ❏ fire-starter kit and paper tinder
- ❏ waterproof matches with striker

FIRST AID
- ❏ 2 antibacterial wipes
- ❏ 2 bandages
- ❏ safety pin or needle

FISHING GEAR
- ❏ artificial bait
- ❏ fishing line
- ❏ 2 hooks
- ❏ 2 sinkers

OPTIONAL ITEMS
- ❏ candle
- ❏ coffee filter
- ❏ duct tape
- ❏ elastic bandage
- ❏ energy bar
- ❏ fingertip wire saw
- ❏ Mylar blanket
- ❏ pencil and paper
- ❏ poncho
- ❏ signaling mirror
- ❏ extra water

GLOSSARY

dehydrated (dee-HYE-dray-tid)—a condition in which a person has not had enough water to drink; symptoms of dehydration include dizziness, headaches, confusion, and fainting

exhaustion (eg-ZAWS-chuhn)—extreme tiredness

forage (FOR-ij)—to search for food

frostbite (FRAWST-bite)—an injury caused to skin by extreme cold, frostbite mostly affects toes, fingers, ears, and noses, and in the worst cases it can lead to the amputation (removal) of damaged body parts

hypothermia (hye-puh-THUR-mee-uh)—a condition in which a person's body temperature drops too low; symptoms of hypothermia include shivering, slurred speech, lack of energy, and clumsiness

microorganisms (mye-kroh-OR-guh-niz-uhmz)—living things, such a bacteria, that are too small to see

observe (uhb-ZURV)—to watch and notice something

signal (SIG-nuhl)—things that attract attention, such as flashing lights or smoke clouds

solar still (SOH-lur STIL)—a tool to get clean water using the heat of the sun

tinder (TIN-dur)—small pieces of flammable material used to start a fire

toxic (TOK-sik)—poisonous or containing something poisonous

READ MORE

Frisch, Nate. *Camping.* Mankato, MN: Creative Education, 2018.

Hoena, Blake. *Could You Escape a Deserted Island?: An Interactive Survival Adventure.* North Mankato, MN: Capstone Press, 2020.

Lake, G. G. *Take Your Pick of Survival Situations.* North Mankato, MN: Capstone Press, 2017.

INTERNET SITES

Boys' Life: How to Build a Survival Shelter
https://boyslife.org/outdoors/3473/taking-shelter/

Outdoor and Wilderness Survival Skills: Lessons for Kids
https://study.com/academy/lesson/outdoor-wilderness-survival-skills-lesson-for-kids.html

Smokey Bear—How to Build Your Campfire
https://smokeybear.com/en/prevention-how-tos/campfire-safety/how-to-build-your-campfire

INDEX

air, 8, 17
animals, 6, 16, 28, 31, 36, 40, 41
avalanches, 17

caves, 16, 17
clothes, 8, 20, 41, 42
compasses, 13, 40, 41

dehydration, 10, 11

exhaustion, 12, 11, 29

fire, 6, 7, 8, 12, 18, 19, 20, 29, 40, 43, 45
fire-starter kits, 18, 19, 43, 45
first aid kits, 32, 34, 42, 45
fishing kits, 31, 43, 45
flags, 41
flares, 38
food, 7, 8, 12, 28, 29, 30–31, 42, 43
foraging, 30–31
frostbite, 10

hypothermia, 10, 11, 20

injuries, 32, 34–35
insects, 31

lean-tos, 17

maps, 13, 42
matches, 7, 18, 45
microorganisms, 23, 25
mirrors, 40, 41
movement, 38
multitools, 9

observation, 6, 14

panic, 4–5
paracord bracelets, 15
plants, 30–31
practice, 42–43

rainwater, 24–25
rescue, 5, 12, 22, 28, 38, 41
rule of three, 8, 22, 28

shade, 6, 10
shelter, 7, 8, 10, 12, 14–15, 16–17, 20, 29, 43
signal fires, 40
signals, 38, 40–41
slings, 37
snacks, 29, 42
snow caves, 17
solar stills, 26–27
SOS messages, 41
splints, 37
sunburn, 6
survival kits, 38, 42, 44–45

tarp shelter, 16, 43
temperature, 6, 10, 12, 11, 17, 20–21, 22
tinder, 18, 19, 45
trails, 4
trench shelter, 17

water, 7, 8, 11, 14, 22, 23, 24–27, 42
water collection, 24–27
water purification, 25, 26
weather, 6, 8, 10, 11, 12, 22
whistles, 41
worms, 31